12
JOURNEYS

To Peace,
Joy &
Fulfillment

ERIC OLANDER

Published by MCM Publishing, a division of Monkey C Media,
MCMPublishing.com

Book Design by Monkey C Media, MonkeyCMedia.com
Edited by Chris Zook, theconsciouswriter.com

Publishing consulting by Karla Olson, BookStudio, BookStudioBooks.com

Dedication

Dedicated to the staff & volunteers

at the San Diego Art Institute.

TABLE OF CONTENTS

Rush

A journey can begin with

just a rush of cool wind that straightens us

and awakens the senses within.

Foreword

12 Journeys reflects many of the core drives found in the writing of Abraham Maslow and the New Wave Movement. The positive, eloquent language of personal growth ushers us into a new world of reflective thought and a stronger connection to the beauty and good around us. We learn to appreciate more the spiritual connections all cultures share. The powerful principles of positive personal change help us follow through with the improvements we wish to make in our outlooks and in the way we interact with our world.

Life presents many unexpected challenges as we progress

toward the fulfillment of our goals. We sometimes put thoughts about personal insight aside as we pursue the needs of work, family, and friends. Together all can play an important role in the way we approach each day.

As we grow as individuals and become more like the person we wish to be and interestingly, sometimes, more like the person we have always been, we sort out the good from the not so good. We can become the person who has worthwhile passions and the will to follow them wisely.

Step with me for a moment into a new world of self expression. We are standing at the top of the stairs in the Museum of the Living Artists in Balboa Park's San Diego Art Institute. For several years I have been drawn down these stairs to experience wonderful art and the care that the Institute's staff takes in its presentation. As we journey down these steps, to one side, we see a sculptural piece- six connected, bright red, half circles- surrounded by the beautiful paintings of the Institute's artists. Levitation has become the first of seven sculptures submitted and accepted for display by the Institute's guest judges.

12 Journeys will help you become more anchored on a purposeful course, endowed with a sense of wonder and appreciation for our world and, yes, empowered to reach goals that will validate your good-will. It will help you to better understand what is really important in living. We all have value and something wonderful to offer; every situation has something positive we can bring to it or take away.

This book was written by a searching, imperfect human being. May you find *12 Journeys* meaningful and useful on your journey. It was written for you.

—Eric Olander

Introduction

Fill your thoughts with harmony. Feel at peace and experience the unity that connects you with the world. Meet life with a heightened sense of well-being. Allow new positive experiences to help shape new constructive outlooks. Achieve a greater sense of meaning and purpose for your life.

When we think about higher awareness as a journey rather than a destination, as an unfolding of experience, we open ourselves to a world of opportunity and growth. We can transform our lives with new, genuine insights. Higher awareness happens as we realize that

Eric Olander

knowledge starts from within and that incredible possibilities lie before us.

The 12 Journeys are founded on the principles of quiet appreciation, self-knowledge, and constructive expressions. The realization that deeper reflection brings about more satisfying life experiences can inspire you to stay on a course of great personal achievement.

The 6 Paths help to clarify the foundations of higher awareness. Practical exercises encourage active participation and offer immediate returns for your efforts. The 6 Fields help to broaden your inquiry and lead you to even more meaningful personal growth and achievement.

Three tools are introduced with the 12 Journeys to support your progress: Affirmations, Visualizations, and Dialogues help you make the changes you feel are important to the journey you undertake. Flexible exercises are included to assist you in reaching your individual objective.

Structured activities enable us to transform our view of ourselves and the way we interact with our world. With 12 Journeys, you determine your own action plan and review your own progress before moving on to a new challenge.

Creating sound objectives is the key to success. Consider progressing from start to finish, one objective at a time. You may, however, wish to develop more than one objective for an individual journey. Stay with a successful strategy. With experience, you may find that developing objectives for two associated journeys at once can bring added efficiency. Keep a notebook record of your progress.

If you decide to target just one or two objectives from the first three journeys, Harmony, Relaxation and Reflection, the experience will bring you real, measurable rewards. You will be gaining new insights and greater peace of mind.

As you grow and overcome obstacles to greater insight, you become more accepting of where you have been. You see the value of the lessons you have learned. You appreciate more the accomplishments you have achieved by your own merit and motivation. Your heart opens as you begin to take solid, practical steps toward renewing a connection with yourself and the world around you.

Start your journey of higher personal consciousness by first seeking meaning in quiet reflection in your own familiar surroundings. Rediscover the fundamental goodness you can find within. Realize the graces in living with a realistic, constructive view of yourself. Develop a strong, personal sense of your identity and extend a message of dignity to everyone you meet.

Structure of
Growth and Change

Real personal growth is assured when we apply the skills of positive affirmation, creative visualization, and constructive dialogues. Use the exercises of 12 Journeys to experience a union of dynamic forces for greater peace of mind, joy, and self-fulfillment.

Great insights begin when we take a closer look at our present situation. By making measured improvements in our current situation and our outlooks, we can achieve a new spirit and a greater clarity of our purposes.

Eric Olander

Affirmations will help strengthen your commitment to improving the way you approach a life situation. *Visualizations* will broaden your creative imagination with positive mental imagery. *Dialogues* will bring you closer to a support network that can help you set goals and solve problems.

12 Journeys also provides examples to help you develop your own structured exercises. Use them individually or develop your own activity plan.

Our focus is on making steady, meaningful progress in our daily lives. Often, our most important achievements involve subtle changes in the pattern of our behavior: the way we approach a task, the way we interact with others, and what we take away from a given situation.

By reviewing our objectives and the relative success of our strategies and their outcomes, we are creating a constructive environment for growth and change.

A gradual, structured course allow us to gather resources, shape positive outlooks, set goals, and make decisions about how to achieve them. When we follow a course that meets our own individual nature, we improve our personal relationship with life and make possible wonderful new experiences.

The most important step in beginning the path of greater awareness is to make a real commitment to learn more about ourselves. Life is unfolding, refining, and perfecting. By using a structured approach and adopting realistic short-term objectives, in very little time we can begin to reach new positive conclusions about ourselves and achieve goals we never thought possible.

Affirmations

Take time to enjoy a pleasant, natural setting for part of your day. So many wonderful things are within our reach, waiting to be recognized and appreciated. Make an affirmation to regularly take time for such quiet moments.

Center your mind in relaxed composure. Direct your thoughts to a good fortune in your life or a gift you have recently given or received. Speak out loud in a positive and confident manner. Directly state a productive outcome you intend to bring about.

You will eventually turn your thoughts to a challenge or a difficulty you may face. Create a positive affirmation to translate these thoughts into a constructive solution to the situation. Great achievements are possible when we focus our efforts toward positive solutions and then take solid steps to reach them.

Your efforts may be uncomfortable at first. It may be difficult to maintain consistency. Try to ensure that your affirmations are meaningful and lasting. Turn them into familiar and resourceful exercises. If necessary, break down an affirmation into gradual steps and reassess and update them on a regular basis. The power of a strong affirmation can result in a great experience.

Preview Exercise

Preview a single affirmation found in the Growth and Change Exercises in any one of the 6 Paths. Think about how you might make the sample affirmation your own. Make a note of your personal interpretation.

Notes

Visualizations

To begin a positive visualization, make yourself comfortable, relax, and close your eyes. Visualize yourself in a familiar setting, practicing a familiar activity. Visualize the beginning, the unfolding, and the successful completion of the action. Then begin and finish the actual task. Finally, review the exercise for clarity of the visualization and take note of the outcome.

It is important to create a scene with enough detail to stimulate the mind. Include color and other sensory information. For greater impact, limit the duration of your visualization. Replay a successful scene, adding new details. Follow through with a constructive action.

By developing the complexity of our visualization gradually, we assure successful outcomes. By being patient and thorough, reviewing our efforts, and revising them when necessary, we ensure consistent growth.

We visualize outcomes and ultimately test them in "real life" situations. Timely revisions help in complex interpersonal situations where outcomes may not be immediate. Being successful is our ultimate motivation.

Preview Exercise

Preview a single Visualization activity found in the Growth and Change Exercises in any one of the 6 Paths or Fields. Think about how you might create a sample Visualization of your own. Make a note of your individual interpretation.

Notes

Dialogues

Dialogues are conversations that help us organize our thoughts. They allow us to gain insights and increase our confidence and commitment. They also place us in a comfortable, supportive environment with stimulating conversation.

We must first accept our situation before we can improve it. We must understand the challenges and obstacles we face. As we seek solutions, we work from the simple to the more complex.

Dialogues help us consider factors we have overlooked. They are most effective when our partners are mature, experienced, and supportive facilitators. They help us turn a challenging situation into a positive experience we can learn from and build upon. A support network of people who can relate to our experiences, share insights, and give assistance is an important asset in achieving our objectives and reaching our goals.

Preview Exercise

Preview a single Dialogue found in the Growth and Change Exercises in any one of the 6 Fields. Think about how you might develop the sample Dialogue on your own. Make a note of your individual interpretation.

Notes

The 6 Paths

The 6 Paths guide you in creating your own personal foundation for higher consciousness. The journey starts from where you are right now. The tools are already within you, ready to expand your horizons and take you to places you know, but may not have experienced in a long time.

Following a structured course, you can make real progress toward greater happiness and personal fulfillment. Higher awareness can come quickly to those who embrace their connection with the life around them.

Take time to unwind and rediscover your capacity for peace and tranquility. Make contact with a natural state of consciousness and harness its dynamic energy. You are on the path of higher awareness when you put yourself in motion, acting with a spirit that cherishes life and living perceptively.

You have unlimited potential to live with a spirit of harmony in your life. Recognize the qualities that make you a unique and valuable individual. Set out on the path of lasting happiness and personal fulfillment.

The Paths provide a set of strategies as starting points for happier, healthier living. Follow each successive Path or progress along a more personally meaningful course. It's all about you making positive choices. Remain resolute in your determination to be successful on your individual journey.

The answers to all your questions lie within you, waiting to be discovered. You need only gather the resources near you and begin your journey of tranquility and greater fulfillment.

Keep a record of your progress and review your experiences to achieve even more favorable results. Your efforts and achievements are part of life's wonderful bigger picture. You will experience real growth as you journey toward a new, brighter destiny for your life.

Harmony

Higher awareness comes when we let stillness and calm restore us. When we focus on living in harmony with our surroundings, we experience a peace and serenity that is vital to our health and sense of well-being. We come closer to the beauty and wonder that exists all around us.

When we open ourselves to the awareness of a world in balance, time slows. We become more open and receptive to the energy that exists in all things. Our senses heighten as we connect with a dynamic energy that empowers us and makes possible great achievement.

As you seek greater self-awareness, be more forgiving of yourself and others. Frame new, positive outlooks and you can discover personal assets and resources you may not even have previously been aware of. New experiences and opportunities will present themselves and become a part of a new, more capable you.

As you open your heart, acknowledge the gifts you have received while looking forward to challenges the future holds. Accept a new vision of yourself and the world around you. Focus on more productive relationships within your family and your community and you will receive the graces of lasting peace of mind and happiness.

"When we let go of how we think things should be and let ourselves flow with life as it presents itself, we come closer to the source of happiness."

–Ilse Klipper

Harmony Exercises

Your Personal Objective —

Growth and Change

Affirm: I appreciate the balance that exists in my life.

Visualize: I see myself working and solving challenging tasks
while maintaining a peaceful perspective on life.

Discuss: I balance harmonious reflections with the
responsibilities of daily living.

Self-Expressions

- Relate when important elements came together to make you joyful and at peace.
- Plan an activity to stimulate feelings of belonging or being connected to the natural environment, your family, or your community.
- Describe a series of events that increased your sense of joy and peacefulness.

Your Objective Review —

Intermediate

Final

Notes

Relaxation

When we relax fully and are peaceful and quiet, tension washes away. We create the conditions for a heightening of our perception. At regular times during the day, sit in a quiet, restful environment. Practice full, even breaths while maintaining good posture. Allow relaxation to develop at its own pace using positive thoughts and images to calm and restore the mind.

As you become more fully in the present, identify worry and stress at their physical, mental, or spiritual source. By becoming centered, at ease, and by systematically relaxing the muscles of the body, you can release tension and begin to create a peaceful frame of mind.

Eric Olander

Relaxation renews our vigor and improves our health. Make a relaxation connection and allow energy to flow through every aspect of your life. Consider taking part in an exercise or activity group. Develop your own library of materials that support increased relaxation and peace of mind.

"The relaxed mind is centered, focused, open, and aware. It is non-judgmental, able to observe without reacting. The relaxed mind is fully in the present, sensitive, and perceptive."

—John Harvey

Relaxation Exercises

Your Personal Objective —

Growth and Change

Affirm: I practice full, even breathing

to achieve more peaceful, relaxed states.

Visualize: I see myself relaxing as tension and stress fall away.

Discuss: Structured relaxation helps me achieve

greater peace of mind.

Self-Expressions

- When and where do you feel most comfortable relaxing?

- List your practices for regular relaxation.

- Describe your feelings or outlooks related to your relaxation activities.

Your Objective Review —

Intermediate

Final

Notes

Reflection

Reflective thinking renews our spirit and guides us in the natural flow of our lives. It leads us to moments of joyful serenity. When we strengthen our commitment to living in harmony, we heighten our senses. We experience more the fullness of our being. We feel the energy flowing within us and through everything that surrounds us.

Reflective thought guides us to greater happiness and self-fulfillment in our lives. We become more aware and in control of our emotional lives. We can better filter out negative thoughts and focus on being more genuine and enthusiastic. The goodness and beauty we feel from within permeates all we experience and undertake.

Strive to be in touch with your true nature and know better your life purposes. Fulfillment comes with self-discovery, carrying a positive attitude, and undertaking inspired activity. Let positive thinking be the source of greater creativity and insight. Stay in touch with your higher self. Allow in only those things that support worthy, core values and a clear vision of the proper course for your life.

"That's what it means to be enlightened. You're not holding onto anything inside. You're inwardly free. Your heart is wide open, and you're already at peace."

—Jim Dreaver

Reflection Exercises

Your Personal Objective —

Growth and Change

Affirm: I am calm and in touch with the

goodness and beauty that surrounds me.

Visualize: I see myself peacefully engaged in reflective thought.

Discuss: Reflective thinking inspires me to greater achievements.

Self-Expressions

- Relate a meaningful early reflection.

- Describe what you most appreciate in quiet reflection.

- What inspiration has resulted from your reflection?

Your Objective Review —

Intermediate

Final

Notes

Voice

Effective speaking clarifies the values of peaceful, harmonious living. When we live with joy and appreciation, we are more in touch with feelings and expressions that influence our relations with others.

By staying positive and self-accepting, we are more open to others. Defensiveness and envy are often masked emotions that limit our growth and opportunities to enrich our experiences.

Fresh insights follow the inner voice that moves us away from upsetting thoughts and emotions.

Be creative in the way you express yourself by being more positive, flexible, and endearing to others. By accepting the expressions of others even when they may differ from your personal viewpoint, you are expanding your own awareness and creating the opportunities to share your own insights. Appreciate your family, your friends, and associates more, and they in turn will be more appreciative of you.

"Insert consciously chosen positive words into your stream of thought. You can create a pattern in your mind and it will be manifested in your life."

—Gay Hendricks

Voice Exercises

Your Personal Objective —

Growth and Change

Affirm: I use constructive language to stay positive

and to be helpful to others.

Visualize: I see myself being supportive in a problem-solving

situation with another.

Discuss: A flexible communication style helps

improve my relationships.

Self-Expressions

- Describe the general tone of your communication.

- What improvements have you sought in a significant relationship?

- What new opportunities have developed out of an improvement in your communication skills?

Your Objective Review —

Intermediate

Final

Notes

Will

The world embraces those who can demonstrate a passion for a worthy cause. We admire their conviction and resolve. We recognize the planning and consistent effort evident in their influence and productivity.

Each step we take toward a principled objective brings us closer to more satisfying life experiences. Be committed to putting your best effort forward. Great insights are gained when you maintain a relaxed state of mind. Explore every significant interest, every resource that can help you to make steady progress on your journey.

Time is on your side when your long-term goals are translated into clear and appropriate objectives. Patience, resilience, and resourcefulness will make you ultimately successful.

"The will is a force like a river that you can flow with or try to swim against. You can use it either to beckon and invite you towards your higher path or to punish you for apparent transgressions."

—Sanaya Roman

Will Exercises

Your Personal Objective —

Growth and Change

Affirm: I will maintain healthy, productive outlooks,

and personal habits.

Visualize: I see myself preparing to meet challenges

and achieve my objectives.

Discuss: A strong resolve makes higher awareness possible.

Self-Expressions

- Identify an interest that gives you a sense of accomplishment.
- Describe a time when you felt like giving up but continued and completed an activity.
- Describe yourself in terms of a desire you have had and its personal effect on you.

Your Objective Review —

Intermediate

Final

Notes

Energy

A positive state of mind has a dramatic effect on our health and energy levels. When we are receptive and appreciative of our world and the opportunities it extends to us, we are enriched and empowered. We experience a heightening of our personal effectiveness. We begin to pursue courses and follow through with actions that ensure greater success in our daily lives.

Take time away from your regular responsibilities and seek a healthy change of pace. New surroundings and new experiences will stimulate and rejuvenate your mind.

Regular exercise can improve our staying power, strength, and flexibility. Organized exercise programs can allow for individualized interests and ability levels. They provide experienced guidance that can help keep us on the right track.

Eric Olander

A balanced diet should include healthy food in the right amounts: breads and cereals, meat, beans and nuts, fruits and vegetables, and dairy products. Start the day with a healthy breakfast. Limit the amount of fats, oils, and sweets you consume.

Put yourself on a course to healthier living. Let proper diet, exercise, and positive outlooks become your wellspring for a more joyful, energetic lifestyle.

"Energy is available to those who are intuitive and healing and on a path of joy. With that energy comes the opportunity to have great abundance and joy right now."

—Sanaya Roman

Energy Exercises

Your Personal Objective —

Growth and Change

Affirm: I am mastering a healthier and more energetic lifestyle.

Visualize: I see myself eating better and exercising more as my

stamina increases.

Discuss: Healthy living increases my energy and confidence.

Self-Expressions

- Identify an influence or motivation that caused you to strive to improve some aspect of your life.

- List the steps you are taking to increase your energy and enthusiasm.

- Describe activities you feel have contributed to your health.

Your Objective Review —

Intermediate

Final

Notes

The 6 Fields

A quiet confidence emerges as you contemplate your place in the world and craft solutions that satisfy your individual interests and aspirations.

Higher awareness brings about many satisfying life experiences and keeps you on a course of discovery and greater achievement. Reconnect with the fundamental goodness you find within.

Realize the grace in living with a positive view of yourself while sending positive messages to those who share your life experiences.

The 6 Fields transform increased self-awareness into dramatic gains in your outlooks and personal effectiveness. By acknowledging and reaffirming the values of reflection and spiritual living, you sustain greater peace of mind and joy in your life.

You bring new clarity and broadened insight to your decision-making. An enlightened awareness makes problem-solving fluid, natural, and sometimes effortless.

Higher consciousness empowers you with new potential for enlightened living. It validates your good will. It is part of the reason why miracles are happening within and all around you right now. As your senses sharpen, your enthusiasm for joyful discovery grows; you engage life with spirited optimism. As one achievement follows another, your tasks will never be fully complete. Your journey of enlightenment will never truly end.

Faith

Spiritual consciousness is a path to greater peace and meaning for our lives. Faith is an enduring journey, ever-expanding and timeless. Appreciate the beauty and abundance that is present all around you, right here and now.

A stronger faith liberates your heart with a soaring spirit, transforming and delivering you to peace and prosperity. You feel a connection and are at one with the energy and light that flows through everything around you. You see without being judgmental. A new awareness puts you at ease and strengthens your resolve to honor and cherish life.

When we accept the symbols and ideals of spiritual wisdom, they become lasting signposts for a life filled with virtue. Their messages are woven into the fabric of human experience which are lessons bound by the truths of humanity's highest consciousness.

As you build greater compassion toward yourself, extend it to all who seek greater meaning in their lives. Offer a helping hand to others and broaden your faith through mutual empowerment. The graces bestowed upon you will be long lasting and full of joy.

"Embark on an inner journey and glimpse the boundless spiritual wealth that is hidden within each of us."

—Ilse Klipper

Faith Exercises

Your Personal Objective —

Growth and Change

Affirm: My faith fills me with purpose and

grants me peace of mind.

Visualize: I see myself strengthened by faith and expressing the

reverence of a spiritual life.

Discuss: Faith is a source of higher awareness.

Self-Expressions

- Describe a spiritual reference that has influenced you.

- Identify how you have received a spiritual message.

- Translate a spiritual insight into a personal lesson.

Your Objective Review —

Intermediate

Final

Notes

Eric Olander

Order

Good organization helps us to distribute our efforts effectively. By maintaining greater order in our lives, we accomplish more and are better able to enjoy our efforts.

Solutions are more accessible when the necessary tools are in their proper places. By establishing priorities, we are making choices that ensure successful outcomes. We are on a satisfying journey.

As we make good use of our time, confidence and productivity expand. We become a part of the network of energy that makes everything possible. We are opening ourselves to new opportunities and rewarding adventures.

As your organizational abilities strengthen, stay on the path of higher awareness. Allow your expectations to soar.

Allow yourself to blend in with the positive interests and abilities of those around you. Effective relationships make for better working conditions for all. Show your appreciation for others. Share the credit for successful outcomes. You will be contributing to the quality of life in a world we all live in.

"Make the desire to be one with the spirit your goal, and all your human desires will come into balance and will be taken care of, one way or another. It's magical how it works."

—Jim Dreaver

Order Exercises

Your Personal Objective —

Growth and Change

Affirm: Being more organized brings me greater peace of mind.

Visualize: I see myself making effective plans and following

through on my commitments.

Discuss: Good organization makes difficult things possible.

Self-Expressions

- Describe how good organization has helped you be more productive.

- Relate an area you have kept organized.

- List some personal objectives and place them in logical order.

Your Objective Review —

Intermediate

Final

Notes

Knowledge

Self-mastery happens when we are in touch with our emotions. When we seek greater awareness of the world around us, we are enriched. As we grow and learn, we open ourselves to new ideas. We encounter truths that inspire our sense of wonder and a greater appreciation for life. When we live earnestly in this way, we are more at ease and at one with ourselves.

When we clarify the things that inspire and challenge us most, our skills increase. We gain confidence as we follow a path of spirited inquiry. We integrate information through gathering, organizing, and analyzing skills. We apply this new knowledge in more practical and efficient ways. We are becoming more confident, resourceful and accomplished as individuals.

As we grow, learn, and prosper, we live with greater peace, joy, and gratitude for our new insight and for all that we are.

"Your life purpose is the most important thing you can get clear on. Clarity of purpose will direct clear energy into every other area of your life. The next level of clarity is clarity of intent, in one sense it is a picture of where you are going or the process you want to experience in getting there."

—Gay Hendricks

Knowledge Exercises

Your Personal Objective —

Growth and Change

Affirm: I commit to learning and achieving greater abilities.

Visualize: I see myself pursuing the knowledge I need

to reach my goals.

Discuss: Learning invites enthusiasm and self-renewal.

Self-Expressions

- Identify the area of learning you are most interested in pursuing.
- Relate something you have learned about yourself and how it translates into a course of self-improvement.
- Describe insights into your ability to maintain good health or a sense of well-being.

Your Objective Review —

Intermediate

Final

Notes

Mind

Our active mind is at the center of our decision-making. It helps us make choices that are healthy, growth-oriented, and self-sustaining. Our active mind can bring us closer to the sources of our emotions and help us to better understand all our motivations.

To improve the functioning of your active mind, rediscover the extraordinary pleasure that can be found in the ordinary experiences of daily life.

Create positive expressions that can help to brighten each and every day. Turn your thoughts to the exploration of a life lived with a spirit of hope and optimism.

A creative mind functions more intuitively when it is in harmony with our everyday linear thinking. It recognizes and appreciates the beauty and good in the world.

Experience more in the present and enjoy moments devoted to peace and serenity. Value your connection to the flow of energy that surrounds and empowers everything.

"When you are tranquil and calm, when you slow down and feel relaxed, you are able to create and think at your higher levels."

—Sanaya Roman

Mind Exercises

Your Personal Objective —

Growth and Change

Affirm: My thoughts are uplifted by a peaceful mind.

Visualize: I see myself free of concerns, seeking tranquility and higher awareness.

Discuss: A spiritual relationship with life reveals balance and harmony in the world.

Self-Expressions

- Relate how an emotion has affected you recently and how you responded to it.

- Describe how balanced, harmonious thinking has helped you be more effective.

- Identify a regular activity that helped you shape more positive feelings and outlooks.

Your Objective Review —

Intermediate

Final

Notes

Love

When we allow the grace of love to enter our lives, we are filled with joy and vitality. We feel an inner peace. We are in touch with the fullness of our being. Our worries are suspended as we free ourselves of negative thoughts and emotions.

As our capacity to love grows, we express greater acceptance and appreciation toward others. We experience moments when love seems to touch all that we encounter. Love broadens our experiences and creates new opportunities for joyful living.

A spiritual voice energizes and guides us when we commit to give of ourselves. Love blossoms in every aspect of our lives. Our thoughts turn to bringing lasting comfort and empowerment to others.

Eric Olander

"You can increase love in your life by looking forward, letting go of your past patterns, and believing in your ability to love even more than you have loved in the past."

—Sanaya Roman

Love Exercises

Your Personal Objective —

Growth and Change

Affirm: I experience the flow of spiritual energy that is the source
of my loving expressions.

Visualize: I see myself extending caring support and love toward
others.

Discuss: I accept a commitment to love and share my life.

Self-Expressions

- Describe a supporting relationship within your family or with a close friend.

- Describe how a loving expression has affected your energy level or frame of mind.

- Express your experience of trust, caring, or appreciation in a significant relationship.

Your Objective Review —

Intermediate

Final

Notes

Power

Personal strength comes with a sense of purpose and an appreciation for a life well lived. It is demonstrated by the individual who is resourceful and who can endure hardships and overcome adversity. Powerful awareness happens when we are committed to a course we can truly believe in. It is open to those who possess faith and energy and can sustain high levels of productive effort.

Address your deepest needs as you set priorities and test them against your idea of a life well lived. Address the physical, material, emotional, and spiritual forces that can bring a vibrant spirit to all you do.

Worthwhile outcomes require extra effort. Maintain good working relationships with others as you acquire the tools and abilities to become more successful.

A positive energy can resonate through you as you accept challenges that lie ahead. Share this energy with those who are close to you. The ability to make a contribution to the well-being of others validates your good nature.

Understand that power is also the ability to express generosity, tolerance, and appreciation for the talents and expressions of the people and life around you.

"We give it the power each moment. What is real is this moment, and you have ultimate choice when you're in it."

—Gay Hendricks

Eric Olander

Power Exercises

Your Personal Objective —

Growth and Change

Affirm: I strive to reach worthwhile goals. I overcome the

hardships that cross my path.

Visualize: I see myself as poised, confident, and productive even in

difficult situations.

Discuss: Higher awareness is a basis of personal power and more

effective relationships with others.

Self-Expressions

- Identify an important source of your personal strength.

- Describe your current planning for reaching a goal.

- Relate how your increased confidence has contributed to recent successful outcomes.

Your Objective Review —

Intermediate

Final

Notes

Selected Quotation Sources

Dreaver, Jim. *The Way of Harmony*. New York: Avon Books, 1999.

Harvey, John, R. *Total Relaxation*. New York: Kodansha International, 1998.

Hendricks, Gay. *Conscious Living*. San Francisco: Harper, 2000.

Klipper, Ilse. *Coming into Harmony*, Palo Alto, CA: Pathways Press, 1992.

Roman, Sanaya. *Living with Joy*. Tiburon, CA: H.J. Kramer Inc., 1986.

Bibliography

Andrews, Frank. *The Art and Practice of Loving*. New York: Penguin Putnam Inc., 1991.

Baker, Douglas, Dr. *Esoteric Psychology, The Seven Rays*. Dallas: Group Dynamics, 1975.

Benson, Herbert, M.D. *The Relaxation Response*. New York: William Morrow & Co., 1975.

Branden, Nathaniel. *The Art of Living Consciously*. New York: Simon & Schuster, 1997.

Brinthaupt, Thomas, and Richard Lipka. *Changing the Self*. New York: State University of New York Press, 1994.

Buscaglia, Leo F. *Living, Loving & Learning*. New York: Ballantine Books, 1962.

Dean, Amy D. *Peace of Mind Daily Meditations for Easing Stress*. New York: Bantam Books, 1995.

Dreaver, Jim. *The Way of Harmony*. New York: Avon Books, 1999.

Dorsman, Jerry, and Bob Davis. *How to Achieve Peace of Mind*. Rocklin, CA: Prima Publishing, 1994.

Dyer, Wayne. *10 Secrets for Success and Inner Peace*. Carlsbad, CA: Hay House Inc.,

Eric Olander

2001.

Frank, Jerome D., M.D. _Persuasion and Healing_. New York: Schocken Books, 1963.

Fortgang, Laura Berman. _Living Your Best Life_. New York: Penguin Putnam Inc., 2001.

George, Mike. _Learn to Relax_. San Francisco: Chronicle Books, 1998.

Gerzon, Robert. _Finding Serenity in the Age of Anxiety_. New York: Bantam Books, 1997.

Goble, Frank. _The Third Force_. New York: Pocket Books, 1971.

Goleman, Daniel. _Emotional Intelligence_. New York: Bantam Books, 1995.

Greenspan, Stanley. _The Growth of the Mind_. Reading, MA: Perseus Books, 1997.

Harvey, John R. _Total Relaxation_. New York: Kodansha International, 1998.

Hendricks, Gay. _Conscious Living_. San Francisco: Harper, 2000.

Klipper, Ilse. _Coming into Harmony_. Palo Alto, CA: Pathways Press, 1992.

LeShan, Lawrence. _How to Meditate_. New York: Bantam Books, 1987.

Maltz, Maxwell. _The Magic Power of Self Image Psychology_. Englewood Cliffs, NJ: Prentice Hall, 1971.

Maslow, Abraham. _Religions, Values, and Peek Experience_. New York: Penguin Press, 1970

McGinnis, Alan Loy. *The Friendship Factor*. Minneapolis, MN: Augsburg Publishing House, 1979.

McKeever, George. *Strategy for Success*. San Diego: McKeever Press, 1993.

Miller, Sherod, PhD. *Straight Talk*. New York: Signet, 1981.

Mramor, Nancy, PhD. *Spiritual Fitness*. St Paul, MN: Llewellyn Publishers, 2004.

Nelsen, Jane. *From Here to Serenity*. Roseville, CA: Prima Publishing, 2000.

Ornstein, Robert E. *The Psychology of Consciousness*. Middlesex, England: Penguin Books LTD, 1972.

Peale, Norman Vincent. *Enthusiasm Makes the Difference*. New York: Fawcett Crest, 1967.

Roland, Paul. *How to Meditate*. China: Octopus Publishing Group Limited, 2000.

Roman, Sanaya. *Living with Joy*. Tiburon, CA: H.J. Kramer Inc., 1986.

White, John. *The Highest States of Consciousness*. New York: Archer Books, 1972.

Zinn, Jon Kabat. *Wherever You Go There You Are*. New York: Hyperion, 1994.

www.ingramcontent.com/pod-product-compliance
Lightning Source LLC
Chambersburg PA
CBHW070531030426
42337CB00016B/2176